Exploring dinosaur times

Dr Brian Knapp

World history

Apatosaurus

Look at this dinosaur. It seems to have feathers at its elbows as well as scales on its body! In this book you will learn not only that some dinosaurs were the biggest things that ever lived, but that they were the ancestors of the birds that now fly around us.

Plateosaurus

Tyrannosaurus rex

Dinosaur footprints.

Dinosaurs timeline

TRIASSIC PERIOD		JURASSIC PERIOD		
220 MYA	**205** MILLION YEARS AGO (MYA)			**144** MYA
	Dilophosaurus	Monolophosaurus		Brachiosaurus Ceratosaurus
Eoraptor	Ichthyosaurus	Megalosaurus Pterodactylus	Diplodocus	Stegosaurus
	Cryolophosaurus		Kentrosaurus Apatosaurus	Allosaurus

Contents

Look up the **bold** words in the glossary on page 32 of this book.

Dinosaurs!

Dinosaurs were a kind of scaly **reptile** that lived on land between 220 and 65 million years ago, but which carried their legs beneath their bodies. Flying reptiles – pterosaurs, and ocean-living reptiles – plesiosaurs and ichthyosaurs – are related, but they were not actually dinosaurs. However, all these dinosaur-like creatures are fascinating and we will include them in this book.

Crocodiles and ancient lizards began in this age, but they are also different from dinosaurs; they walk with their legs against the sides of their bodies and have different kinds of bones.

This is a pack of hunting dinosaurs. These are called Aucasaurus. They were not an especially large kind of dinosaur; they were just 4 m long and 1 m high at the hip. They weighed 700 kg. In packs, however, they must have been fearsome. Many of Aucasaurus' relatives had bull-like horns. But we have no idea what the colour of their skin was. As with all of the dinosaur illustrations you will ever see, the colours are artists' guesses and usually similar to modern lizards.

Did you know… ?

- Dinosaurs developed rapidly 220 million years ago after many other creatures died out in a **global catastrophe**.
- Dinosaurs may have been warm-blooded, whereas modern reptiles are cold-blooded.
- Dinosaurs ran with their heads down. They lifted their heads to attack.

Q Why would small dinosaurs hunt in packs?

How are fossils formed?

As you know, flesh normally decays very quickly and bones are eaten by scavengers. But under special circumstances the process can slow right down. This happens, for example, if animals (or plants) are buried in mud and sand during a flood. If remains are buried quickly, the body is buried without being eaten or broken up by wind or waves.

Even when they are preserved in this way, the bones of the dead animals and the tissues of dead plants still change over time. In this way they are changed to 'stone'. They have become **fossils**. Many fossil minerals are harder than the rocks they are in.

We see these fossils if they are found in quarries, or exposed by the wearing away of rocks in cliffs or river banks. Even then, it is only by chance that the fossil is discovered. Most fossils are washed away during floods, or destroyed by quarrying and never seen again.

A fossil skull of a hunting dinosaur.

Did you know... ?

- As bones turn to stone they become heavier.
- That fossil bones can be so delicately preserved that you can see the blood vessels.
- That plants usually change into carbon – we call beds of fossil plants coal.

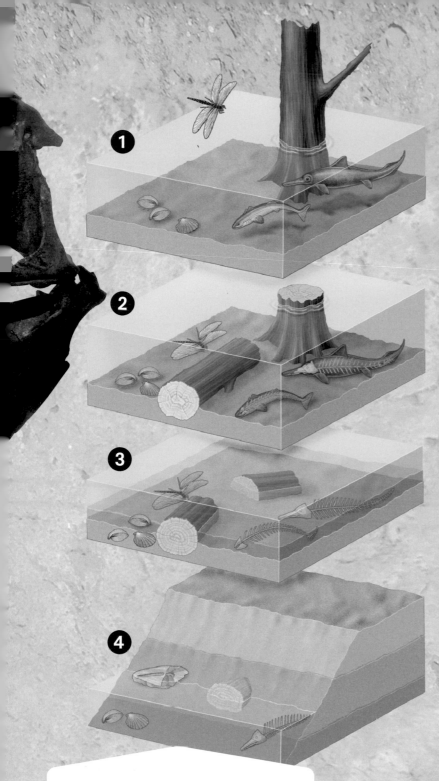

These footprints were made by a dinosaur walking over mud. The impressions dried out and hardened. A flood came along and filled the impressions with sand or silt, and then buried the whole lot in more sand and silt. Gradually it all turned into rock. Now rivers are stripping the rock away and washing the sand and silt out of the footprints, so they look almost as they would have 150 million years ago.

The ones to the right are moulds. The one below is a cast. The very bottom picture is a fossil pile of dinosaur poo! It is called a coprolite.

This diagram shows the events that led to fossils forming.
1 We start with a shallow lake full of plants and animals.
2 Animals and trees die and begin to decay. **3** They start to be buried by sand and mud and some of their remains turn into fossils.
4 Finally, the fossils are exposed millions of years later as the rocks are cut into by rivers.

Q What is the difference between a mould and a cast?

Arm

Backbone
and neck

Pelvis

Rib cage

Hand

Hip

Making sense of the bones

Just occasionally, as shown here, all the fossil bones of a dinosaur stay together as a complete skeleton, more or less as they would have been in real life. This is a small dinosaur with its head bent back towards its tail, but otherwise looking almost as it might hundreds of millions of years ago.

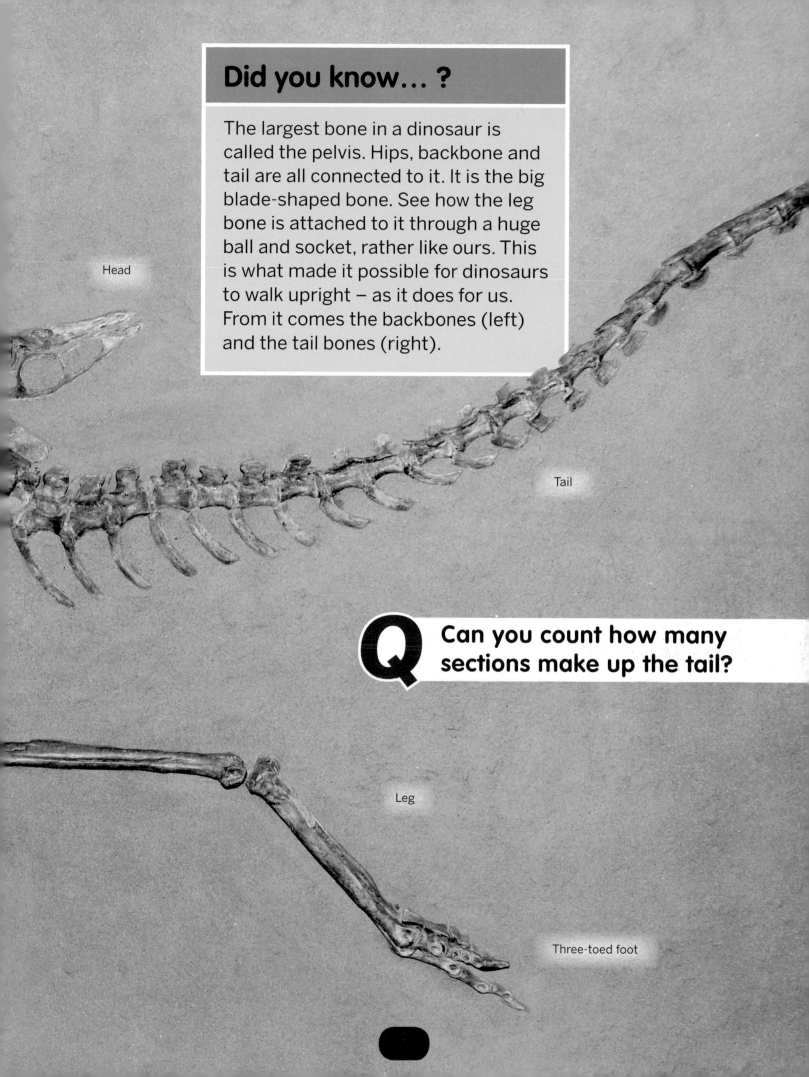

Did you know... ?

The largest bone in a dinosaur is called the pelvis. Hips, backbone and tail are all connected to it. It is the big blade-shaped bone. See how the leg bone is attached to it through a huge ball and socket, rather like ours. This is what made it possible for dinosaurs to walk upright – as it does for us. From it comes the backbones (left) and the tail bones (right).

Head

Tail

Q **Can you count how many sections make up the tail?**

Leg

Three-toed foot

Dino eggs

Many creatures lay eggs, from turtles to birds to crocodiles. Dinosaurs are related to all of these.

Some dinosaurs laid eggs in groups, like turtles. Others dug many pits and laid an egg in each one. This tells us that dinosaurs took a lot of care over their eggs, so they probably stayed with the nest to guard the eggs, too.

Dinosaur eggs are big, but they are not enormous. The bigger the egg, the thicker its shell needs to be in order not to break due to the weight of the baby inside.

Most dinosaur eggs hatched, or were dug up and eaten by other dinosaurs, so there are few fossil eggs or nests. But in a few cases they have been left undisturbed because they were buried by floods or other events. Once buried, the eggs gradually turned into fossils.

The shell was hardly changed, as it was already a **mineral**, but the inside was rarely preserved.

Did you know… ?

- Shells have tiny holes in them called pores. These allowed the baby to breathe. The same pores allowed water and minerals inside during fossilisation.
- Dinosaur eggs could not have been too big or the shell would have been too thick for the baby to break.
- The giant plant-eating dinosaurs laid the biggest eggs – 18 cm long and with shells up to 5 mm thick. The egg inside would have been 5 litres!
- Hunting dinosaurs, like T. rex, would have had eggs 10–15 cm long and a couple of millimetres thick.

Q Was a dinosaur's egg the same shape as a chicken's egg?

Battles of the titans

A few dinosaurs were no bigger than turkeys, but most were large and some were gigantic. Elephants would have been dwarfed by them.

Why did plant-eating dinosaurs become so big? One reason might be the food they had to eat. In dinosaur times the plants were mainly tough-leaved ferns and coniferous trees. They were not as nourishing as modern plants, and they needed tough guts to digest them. The bigger the animal, the longer its gut and the better it could get the nourishment it needed.

Meat is easier to digest and so the hunting dinosaurs did not need to be so big just to digest their food. But their food was the huge plant-eaters, so the bigger the hunter, the more successful it might have been.

Hunting dinosaurs, such as this Suchomimus, were up to 12 m long.

Triceratops was a plant-eater and much bigger than most hunters. It defended itself using its size and huge bony head.

Did you know… ?

- Most healthy grown-up plant-eating dinosaurs could see off the hunting dinosaurs, either by herding together, running fast or just being gigantic.
- Hunters probably ate the young, the ill and the old.
- Hunters may have needed to roam over vast **territories** just to find enough food. They may have needed to be ferocious and shown a face full of sharp teeth just to protect these territories.

 Why was armour useful to the plant-eating dinosaurs?

The gigantic plant-eaters

The biggest dinosaurs were the largest animals ever to live on land. They were plant-eaters. Famous giants included Diplodocus, Apatosaurus (which used to be called Brontosaurus) and Brachiosaurus.

Did you know... ?

- The biggest plant-eaters were part of a group called **sauropods**. Although they were toughly built, the vast bodyweight of the sauropods meant that, most likely, once they grew up, they could never lie down, for their legs would not have the strength to get them off the ground again. So they probably locked their legs and went to sleep standing up.

Long tail

Some plant-eaters (like Plateosaurus, shown here) walked on two legs, while others walked on all fours. They mostly had enormously long necks which they balanced with gigantic tails. They only had small heads.

Q **How did dinosaurs balance the weight of their long necks?**

Small head

Long neck

Barrel-shaped body

Five toes

Apatosaurus

Apatosaurus means 'deceptive lizard' (it was also once called Brontosaurus). It was over 20 m long and weighed up to 25 tonnes.

Apatosaurus was a tough guy. It was more heavily built than its other large relatives, such as Diplodocus, and had a whip-like tail.

Apatosaurus has often been shown with its neck and head held high in the air, but scientists have examined the neck bones and now believe it would have done this rarely. Most of the time it kept its head bent down. If its head had been too high for too long, its heart would have had trouble pumping blood to its brain!

Its lungs moved huge volumes of air in and out with each breath. This is different to a true reptile – reptiles don't breathe as much as most other animals. Instead dinosaur lungs were more like a scaled up size of the lungs birds have. With a bird-like lung system, it would have been able to walk long distances and even break out into a long-distance run, something else that reptiles cannot do.

Diplodocus

Diplodocus had four stump-like legs and a whip-like tail, but it was much more slender. Its limbs were about the same size, so its body was largely held horizontal. The biggest may have been over 50 m long and weighed over 50 tonnes.

Diplodocus probably used its teeth to strip leaves from branches. Diplodocus did not chew its food. The food slipped down into the stomach where it was ground up by stones that the animal ate. This released the nourishment. Of course, what goes in must come out, and Diplodocus dropped a tonne of dung a day, some of which are preserved as fossils called coprolites.

Brachiosaurus

Brachiosaurus means 'arm lizard'. Its front limbs were longer than the back, so it sloped back towards its rump (something like a giraffe does). Brachiosaurus was 25 metres long and the top of its head would have reached 13 metres or more above the ground. It probably weighed about 30 tonnes.

Brachiosaurus must have been an amazing eater. Just to keep itself alive it would have had to eat about 200 kg of food a day (equal to 25 sacks of potatoes).

Frills and plates

In the later stages of dinosaur times, a group of plant-eating dinosaurs developed with beaks and huge bony frills behind their heads. They eventually became the most common dinosaur on the planet.

They grew to 9 m long and weighed nearly 6 tonnes. These monsters were called Zuniceratops, Nedoceratops and Triceratops.

Modern lizards use the frills and crests when they are courting and also when they are trying to protect their territory from others. Perhaps dinosaurs did the same, although no-one knows for sure.

Zuniceratops was a typical bony-frilled dinosaur. See its relation, Triceratops on page 13.

Did you know... ?

- Some of these dinosaurs had heads that made up about a third of their body length.
- Many had tails that could be moved very quickly, just like a whip.

The name Stegosaurus comes from the Greek for 'roof-lizard', named after the very distinctive plates across its back. This Stegosaurus model shows the plates on the top of its spine. No living creature has anything like these, so they remain a mystery. Some people have suggested that they were covered in skin and blood vessels and used to steady the body temperature. Other people think they were for display. It had metre-long spikes on its tail and we can be pretty sure that they were used to swipe from side to side to defend itself from attack.

It was a plant-eater with stubby teeth, so it would not have been a particularly ferocious dinosaur. The skeleton and the reconstruction let you see how the 'flesh' has been put on the bones.

Q **What did Stegosaurus do with its spiked tail?**

Tyrannosaurus rex

Tyrannosaurus means 'tyrant lizard'. It is the name of a group of related animals of which the most famous is Tyrannosaurus rex (*rex* means 'king'). The shortened, or simple, version is T. rex. Many hunting dinosaurs belonged to a group called **theropods**.

Tyrannosaurus rex was the most common large hunting dinosaur at the end of dinosaur times, and its bones are more common than almost any other kind. Tyrannosaurus rex was covered with the pebbly scales common in most dinosaurs. Tyrannosaurus rex had tiny front limbs compared with its gigantic rear limbs. It also had a massive head about 1.5 m long.

It grew up to 13 m long and was 4 m tall at the hips. It weighed about 7 tonnes. However, many of its bones were hollow, so it probably weighed less than people once thought.

Tyrannosaurus rex was like a giant see-saw, using its hips to balance the weight of its great head against that of its long tail.

Tyrannosaurus rex, rearing up on its hind legs to attack. For most of the time, however, it probably held its body more horizontal, as shown on the following pages.

Its eyes were set far apart and facing forwards so it had eyesight that was possibly as good as a modern hawk.

That would be useful for spotting prey in the distance. Mostly, however, Tyrannosaurus rex was probably a scavenger, eating up recently dead plant-eaters. It had a very sensitive nose – able to smell rotting carcasses from a long way off.

Tyrannosaurus rex may have been able to run when it was young, but as it grew up this would have become more and more difficult. Elephants have the same problem. But although Tyrannosaurus rex didn't run, it 'walked' fast and may have reached 40 km an hour. If so, it would have been the fastest large dinosaur.

The backward-sloping teeth stopped any prey from slipping out of its massive bite.

T. rex grew 'slowly' at first. It was less than 2 tonnes even at the age of 14. Then it grew amazingly quickly. It put on 600 kg a year for the next four years, then slowed down again. By this time it was an adult.

Many T. rex seem to have died about 6 years after becoming fully grown, so the animal may not have had a long natural life.

Q How old was T. rex when it died?

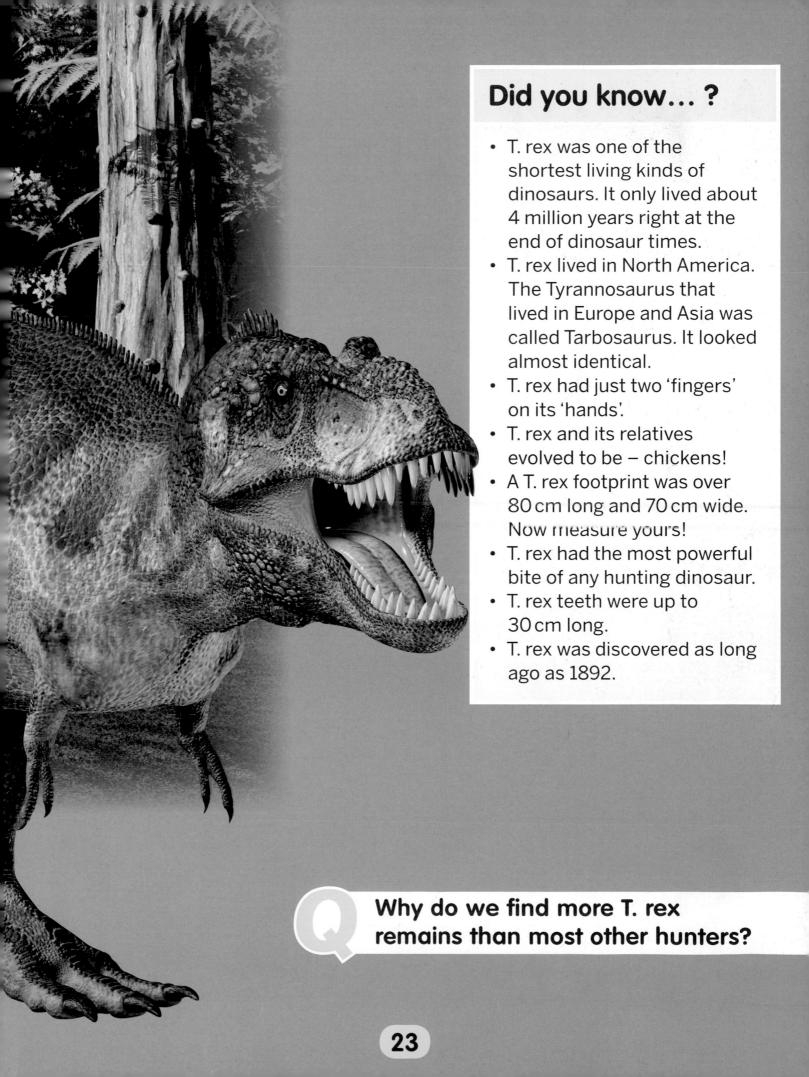

Did you know… ?

- T. rex was one of the shortest living kinds of dinosaurs. It only lived about 4 million years right at the end of dinosaur times.
- T. rex lived in North America. The Tyrannosaurus that lived in Europe and Asia was called Tarbosaurus. It looked almost identical.
- T. rex had just two 'fingers' on its 'hands'.
- T. rex and its relatives evolved to be – chickens!
- A T. rex footprint was over 80 cm long and 70 cm wide. Now measure yours!
- T. rex had the most powerful bite of any hunting dinosaur.
- T. rex teeth were up to 30 cm long.
- T. rex was discovered as long ago as 1892.

Q **Why do we find more T. rex remains than most other hunters?**

A world of terrifying teeth

For a long time, people imagined that hunters moved fast and caught their prey out on the plains, like a lion catching an antelope. However, we now know that grown-up hunting dinosaurs could not run as fast as was once thought. Most adult hunters probably lay in ambush for their prey or ate slow-moving young, older or infirm prey. They would also have been **scavengers** of dead dinosaurs. But even for this, as well as defending their territory, they needed mouths full of terrifying teeth.

Q Where are the spines in Spinosaurus?

Spinosaurus

Although Tyrannosaurus was the most common hunting dinosaur at the end of dinosaur times, it only existed for a fairly short time and it was not even the largest hunter to have lived. Spinosaurus was much longer and heavier.

Spinosaurus is named after the great row of spines down its back. These spines were 2 m long! All of the spines were covered in skin, just as your backbone is covered in skin, and in the case of Spinosaurus it would have made the animal appear to have a great flap, called a sail, on its back.

Spinosaurus lived in Africa from 100 to 93 million years ago. It was 18 m long and weighed 9 tonnes, making it probably the largest hunting dinosaur that ever lived. It had one of the longest heads – about 2 m – of any hunting dinosaur. Its jaws were filled with straight conical teeth.

It may well have been a fishing dinosaur because Its nostrils are high up on its nose (like a crocodile), but again, like a crocodile, it would probably have eaten anything that came within reach!

Did you know... ?

- Young hunting dinosaurs were much more agile than the adults. As they grew up they became so heavy, they slowed down.
- Spinosaurus was the main fearsome dinosaur of *Jurassic Park III*. It was also shown with T. rex, but, in reality, these animals never lived on the same continent and they lived millions of years apart.

Allosaurus

Allosaurus means 'strange lizard'. It had a double crest on its head. It was a large dinosaur that lived 155 to 145 million years ago. It probably grew to 12 m long and was about 10 m tall.

Allosaurus had huge legs (hind limbs) and tiny arms (forelimbs). Its inner ear was similar to a crocodile, so it probably made, and heard, low sounds. It had a good sense of smell, well suited for tracking down dead animals. It lived for up to 30 years, quite similar to other large hunters.

Young Allosaurus were much more agile than adults, and probably hunted in packs. But, as they became older, heavier and slower, they may have become more solitary, protecting their own territory from other Allosauruses and settling down to ambushing prey instead of chasing it, or simply scavenging the carcasses of other animals they happened to chance by.

Hunters galore

All of the hunting dinosaurs had huge heads and terrifying teeth, but there were many differences in size, shape and weight. You can see that here.

Monolophosaurus

Monolophosaurus means 'one-crested lizard'. It was a hunter from the Jurassic. The first specimens were found as recently as 1984. It was 5 m long, 2 m high and weighed a tonne. Monolophosaurus is thought to be related to Allosaurus.

Cryolophosaurus

Cryolophosaurus means 'cold crest lizard'. It was 6 to 8 metres long. It had a huge crest which ran across, not along, its head above its eyes, making it look like a comb. Because it looked like the hair style of rock-and-roll singer Elvis Presley, this dinosaur got the nickname 'Elvisaurus' when it was first discovered in 1991.

Cryolophosaurus is the only dinosaur to have been found in what is now the freezing wastes of Antarctica. It was found with fossilised tree trunks, telling us that Antarctica used to be much warmer than it is today.

Ceratosaurus

Ceratosaurus means 'horned lizard' because it had a bony horn on its snout and a pair of bony projections over its eyes. Ceratosaurus was smaller but somewhat similar to Allosaurus. It was 8 m long, under 3 m at the hip, and weighed just a tonne. It could live alongside Allosaurus because it could swim, and so it got its food by hunting in rivers.

Q Which was nicknamed the Elvis Presley dinosaur?

Fishers of the deep

The great ocean-living reptiles were not dinosaurs, but they lived and died at the same time and they were equally spectacular.

Ichthyosaur is Greek for 'fish lizard'. For tens of millions of years ichthyosaurs were the masters of the oceans. Then they became extinct and their place was taken by a new group called plesiosaurs.

Did you know… ?

- Ichthyosaurs looked a bit like fish and dolphins but were in no way related. Fish were their food. They needed the same shape to get about in the water.
- Ichthyosaurs could swim at up to 40 km/hr.
- Plesiosaurs developed large flippers, sometimes called paddles.

Elasmosaurus was a plesiosaur with an extremely long neck. It lived 65 million years ago. It was about 14 m long and weighed 2 tonnes. Half of its length was neck. It had a small head with many sharp teeth. Its neck was too weak to allow it to rear up out of the water (as in some popular films).

An ichthyosaur skeleton. The shading shows you what the real shape with flesh looked like. Notice the fin on its back.

Q **What did an ichthyosaur eat?**

Masters of the skies

Many people know the ancient flying reptiles as 'pterodactyls' but, actually, the name for flying reptiles is pterosaur. Pterodactyl is a name only for short-tailed pterosaurs.

Did you know… ?

- Pterosaurs, meaning 'winged lizards', lived through the whole of dinosaur times.
- The early pterosaurs were small and lived in trees.
- They were the first animals with backbones to be able to fly.
- Their wings were made of skin stretching from the throat to a hugely lengthened fourth finger.
- Many had long tails and long jaws filled with sharp teeth.
- Pterosaurs were the first animals to have truly hollow bones (like the bones of modern birds) which helped to reduce their weight and so make it easier for them to fly.
- When on the ground, most pterosaurs walked on all fours. Those with small feet most likely needed to walk on firm ground, while those with large feet could have been shallow-water waders.
- Pterosaurs protected their eggs from other reptiles by burying them in the ground, much as crocodiles do.

Pterodactylus

This was a hunter and probably preyed upon fish and other small animals. It was a relatively small pterosaur, only 2.5 m across its wings. It had a crest on its skull, long claws, and the back of its neck was covered with hair. It had webbed feet.

Pteranodon

Pteranodon was one of the largest pterosaurs, growing up to 9 m from wing tip to wing tip. Pteranodon had a crest on its head and a toothless beak, similar to those of modern birds. It would have flown in a soaring manner rather like a modern-day albatross. When on the ground it could have walked on all fours or just on hind legs. It may also have been able to swim.

How did pterosaurs move about on the ground?

Glossary

Cretaceous, Jurassic, Triassic Names for the three parts of Earth history in which dinosaurs lived. The Triassic started 220 million years ago, then came the Jurassic, and the Cretaceous ended 65 million years ago, and with it the dinosaurs.

fossil The remains of an ancient living thing whose shape has been preserved in rocks. Most, or all, of the once living thing has been changed to new materials, often including the bones.

global catastrophe A time when something very important happened to change the world's climate. Dinosaur times may have begun and ended with a meteorite or comet hitting the Earth.

mineral The materials of which stone is made.

reptile Cold-blooded animals that lay eggs and which have scaly skin. Dinosaurs were probably not really reptiles as there is some evidence that they were warm-blooded.

sauropods A group name for many of the giant plant-eating dinosaurs.

scavenger An animal that eats dead bodies. They are a very important part of a food chain.

territory The space a living thing needs to find enough food to live. Hunting animals may need thousands of square kilometres each, so there will be fewer hunters in an area than plant-eaters.

theropod A group name for many of the giant hunting (meat-eating) dinosaurs.

Index

Curriculum Visions

Curriculum Visions Explorers

This series provides straightforward introductions to key worlds and ideas.

You might also be interested in

Our slightly more detailed 64 pp book, 'A dinosaur life'. All of our products are suitable for KS2.

Dedicated Web Site

Watch movies, see many more pictures and read much more in detail about dinosaurs and other topics:

www.curriculumvisions.com

(It's my turn! and the Learning Centre are subscription areas of the web site)

A CVP Book
Copyright © 2010 Atlantic Europe Publishing

The right of Brian Knapp to be identified as the author of this work has been asserted by him in accordance with the Copyright, Designs and Patents Act 1988.

Author
Brian Knapp, BSc, PhD

Senior Designer
Adele Humphries, BA

Editor
Gillian Gatehouse

Photographs
The Earthscape and Shutterstock Picture Libraries.

Designed and produced by
Atlantic Europe Publishing

Printed in China by
WKT Company Ltd

Exploring dinosaur times – Curriculum Visions
A CIP record for this book is available from the British Library
ISBN 978 1 86214 612 9

This product is manufactured from sustainable managed forests. For every tree cut down at least one more is planted.